LION:

A LION'S ROAR CAN BE HEARD UP TO 5 MILES AWAY!

ELEPHANT:
ELEPHANTS USE THEIR TRUNKS LIKE STRAWS TO DRINK WATER AND PICK UP FOOD.

LEOPARD: LEOPARDS ARE AMAZING CLIMBERS AND LOVE TO NAP IN TREES.

RHINO:
A GROUP OF RHINOS IS CALLED A "CRASH," EVEN THOUGH THEY'RE GENTLE GRAZERS MOST OF THE TIME.

BUFFALO:

BUFFALOS STICK TOGETHER IN GROUPS
TO HELP KEEP EACH OTHER SAFE.

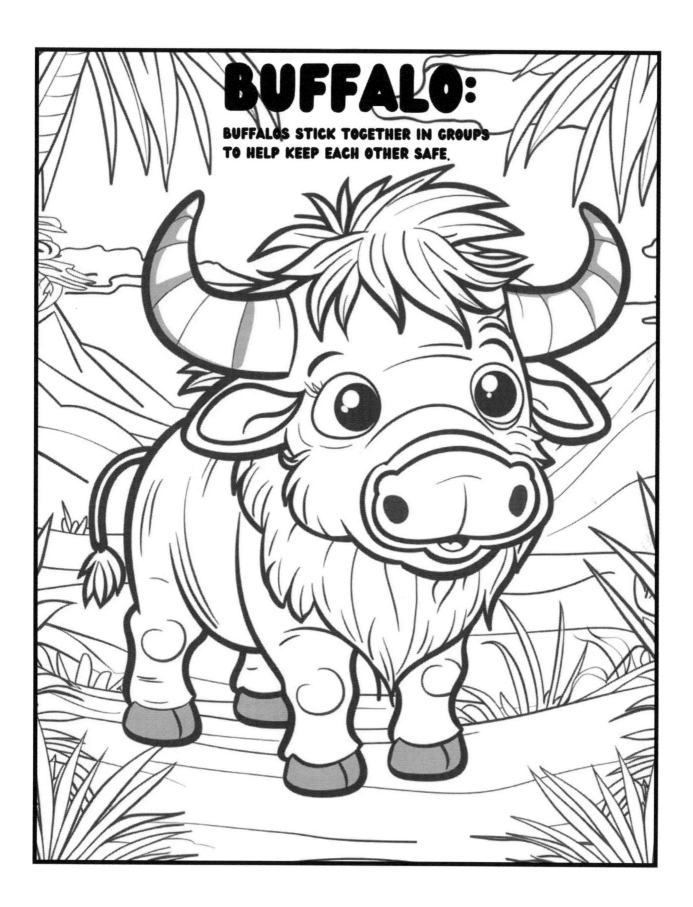

CHEETAH:

CHEETAHS ARE THE FASTEST LAND ANIMALS AND CAN RUN UP TO 70 MPH

ZEBRA: EACH ZEBRA HAS A UNIQUE PATTERN OF STRIPES, LIKE FINGERPRINTS!

HIPPO:

HIPPOS SECRETE A NATURAL SUNSCREEN THAT LOOKS PINK!

WARTHOG: WARTHOGS KNEEL ON THEIR FRONT KNEES TO EAT GRASS.

HYENA:

HYENAS "LAUGH" WHEN THEY'RE EXCITED OR WANT TO TELL THEIR FRIENDS SOMETHING.

ANTELOPE:

SOME ANTELOPES CAN JUMP UP TO 10 FEET HIGH IN ONE LEAP.

BABOON:

BABOONS LIVE IN GROUPS CALLED "TROOPS" AND TAKE TURNS KEEPING WATCH FOR DANGER.

CHIMPANZEE:

CHIMPANZEES USE TOOLS, LIKE STICKS, TO FISH TERMITES OUT OF MOUNDS.

GORILLA: GORILLAS BUILD NESTS OUT OF LEAVES AND BRANCHES TO SLEEP IN EVERY NIGHT.

MONKEY:

SOME MONKEYS, LIKE CAPUCHINS, USE ROCKS TO CRACK OPEN NUTS.

MEERKAT:

MEERKATS HAVE DARK PATCHES AROUND THEIR EYES TO REDUCE GLARE FROM THE SUN, HELPING THEM SEE BETTER.

OSTRICH:

OSTRICHES ARE THE LARGEST BIRDS IN THE WORLD, AND EVEN THOUGH THEY CAN'T FLY, THEY CAN RUN UP TO 45 MILES PER HOUR!

AFRICAN WILD DOG:

AFRICAN WILD DOGS HAVE BIG PACKS AND WORK AS A TEAM WHEN HUNTING, SHARING FOOD AFTERWARD.

JACKAL:

JACKALS ARE OMNIVORES, WHICH MEANS THEY EAT BOTH PLANTS AND MEAT, DEPENDING ON WHAT'S AVAILABLE.

CROCIDILE:

CROCODILES CAN HOLD THEIR BREATH UNDERWATER FOR OVER AN HOUR AND HAVE SUPER-STRONG JAWS WITH MORE THAN 60 TEETH!

MONGOOSE:

MONGOOSES ARE IMMUNE TO SOME SNAKE VENOM, MAKING THEM EXCELLENT SNAKE HUNTERS.

AFRICAN CIVET:

CIVETS HAVE SCENT GLANDS THEY USE TO MARK THEIR
TERRITORY, KIND OF LIKE LEAVING A "SMELL MESSAGE."

SERVAL:

SERVALS HAVE EXTRA-LONG EARS TO HELP THEM HEAR SMALL ANIMALS MOVING IN THE GRASS.

BAT-EARED FOX:

BAT-EARED FOXES HAVE HUGE EARS TO HELP THEM
HEAR INSECTS UNDERGROUND.

AARDVARK:

AARDVARKS HAVE LONG, STICKY TONGUES TO SLURP UP TERMITES.

AARDWOLF:

AARDWOLVES EAT UP TO 300,000 TERMITES IN A SINGLE NIGHT!

PANGOLIN:

PANGOLINS ARE THE ONLY MAMMALS COVERED IN PROTECTIVE SCALES AND CURL UP INTO A BALL WHEN SCARED.

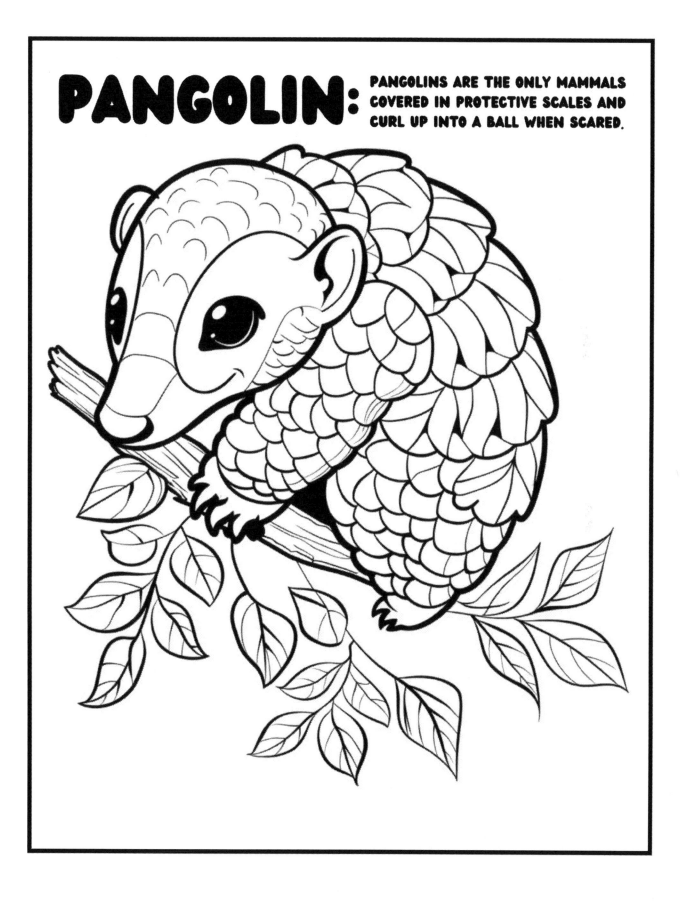

BUSHBABY:

BUSHBABIES HAVE HUGE EYES THAT
HELP THEM SEE IN THE DARK.

HONEYBADGER:

HONEY BADGERS HAVE THICK SKIN THAT HELPS PROTECT THEM FROM BEE STINGS AND OTHER ANIMALS.

REEDBUCK:

REEDBUCKS USE HIGH-PITCHED WHISTLES TO ALERT OTHERS OF DANGER.

HARTEBEEST:

HARTEBEESTS HAVE
SPECIALLY SHAPED HORNS
THAT HELP PROTECT THEIR
HEADS DURING FIGHTS.

AFRICAN RABBIT:

AFRICAN RABBITS ARE NOCTURNAL AND RELY ON THEIR HEARING TO DETECT PREDATORS.

BONGO:

BONGOS HAVE STRIKING WHITE STRIPES THAT HELP THEM CAMOUFLAGE IN FORESTS.

ROCK HYRAX:

EVEN THOUGH ROCK HYRAXES ARE SMALL, THEY ARE RELATED TO ELEPHANTS!

TREE HYRAX:

TREE HYRAXES MAKE
FUNNY SQUEAKY SOUNDS
TO TALK TO EACH OTHER.

ELEPHANT SHREW:

ELEPHANT SHREWS HAVE LONG NOSES THAT LOOK LIKE TINY TRUNKS.

GERENUK:

GERENUKS ARE CALLED "GIRAFFE GAZELLES" BECAUSE OF THEIR LONG NECKS.

NYALA:
NYALA MALES LOOK VERY DIFFERENT FROM FEMALES, WITH DARK FUR AND SPIRAL HORNS.

FLAMINGO:

FLAMINGOS GET THEIR PINK COLOR FROM EATING TINY SHRIMP AND ALGAE.

STORK:

STORKS OFTEN MIGRATE
THOUSANDS OF MILES EACH YEAR.

VULTURE:

VULTURES HELP CLEAN UP NATURE BY EATING ANIMALS THAT WOULD MAKE OTHER ANIMALS SICK.

KESTREL:
KESTRELS CAN HOVER IN MIDAIR LIKE A HELICOPTER AND SEE ULTRAVIOLET LIGHT WHICH HELPS THEM FIND TRAILS OF SMALL ANIMALS.

FALCON:

PEREGRINE FALCONS ARE THE FASTEST ANIMALS IN THE WORLD WHEN DIVING, REACHING SPEEDS OVER 200 MPH.

OWL:

AN OWL'S EYES DON'T MOVE, BUT IT CAN TURN
ITS HEAD ALMOST ALL THE WAY AROUND TO SEE.

SECRETARY BIRD:

SECRETARY BIRDS
USE THEIR LONG
LEGS TO STOMP
ON SNAKES AND
OTHER PREY.

KORI BUSTARD:

KORI BUSTARDS ARE AMONG THE HEAVIEST FLYING BIRDS.

SPURFOWL:

SPURFOWLS DIG IN THE DIRT WITH THEIR STRONG FEET TO FIND SEEDS AND INSECTS.

NILE MONITOR:

NILE MONITORS CAN STAY UNDERWATER FOR UP TO AN HOUR WHILE HUNTING.

AFRICAN TORTOISE:

AFRICAN TORTOISES CAN LIVE OVER 70 - 150 YEARS IN THE WILD!

CHAMELEON:

CHAMELEONS CHANGE COLORS TO MATCH THEIR SURROUNDINGS AND CAN MOVE THEIR EYES INDEPENDENTLY OF EACH OTHER.

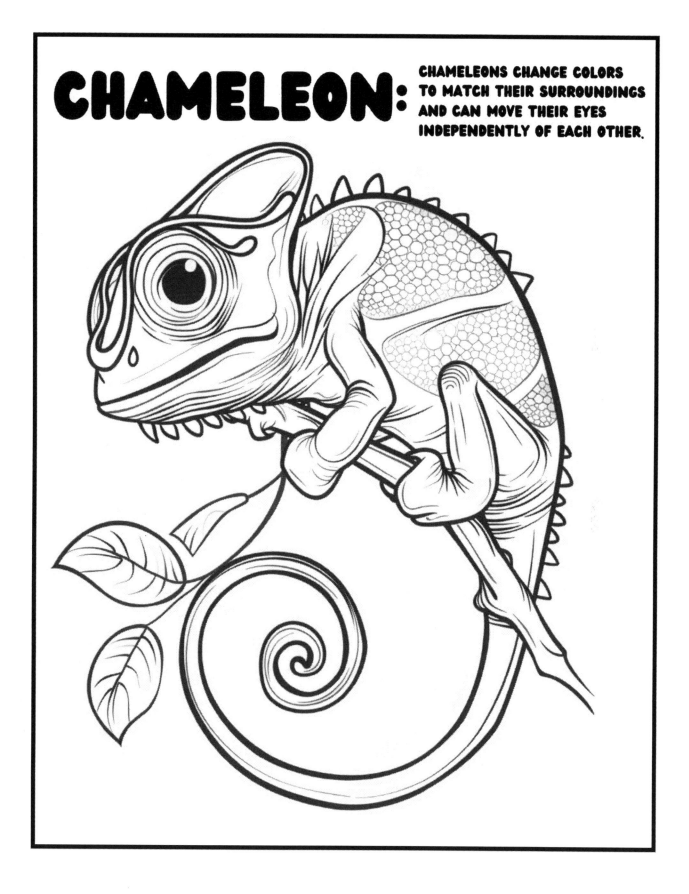

PYTHON:

PYTHONS ARE NON-VENOMOUS SNAKES KNOWN FOR THEIR POWERFUL SQUEEZING ABILITY.

AGAMA LIZARD:

MALE AGAMAS CAN TURN BRIGHT ORANGE OR BLUE DURING
MATING SEASON TO IMPRESS FEMALE LIZARDS.

CLAWLESS OTTER:

CLAWLESS OTTERS USE THEIR SENSITIVE PAWS TO FEEL AROUND FOR FOOD LIKE CRABS AND FISH IN THE WATER!

WHISTLING DUCK:

WHISTLING DUCKS GET THEIR NAME BECAUSE THEY MAKE HIGH-PITCHED WHISTLING SOUNDS INSTEAD OF REGULAR DUCK QUACKS!

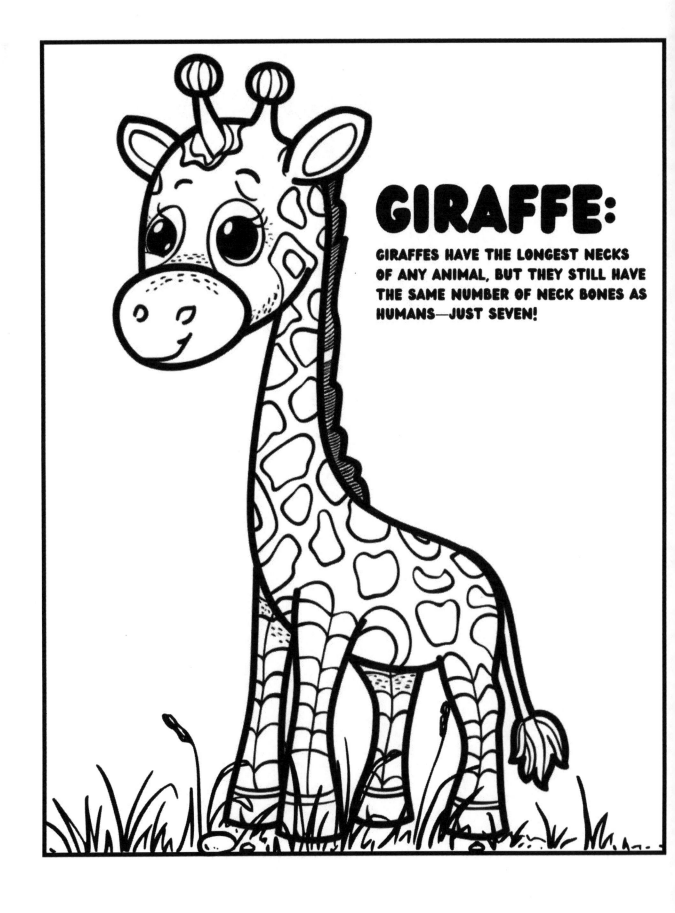

GIRAFFE:

GIRAFFES HAVE THE LONGEST NECKS OF ANY ANIMAL, BUT THEY STILL HAVE THE SAME NUMBER OF NECK BONES AS HUMANS—JUST SEVEN!

BUSH SQUIRREL:

BUSH SQUIRRELS USE THEIR TAILS AS UMBRELLAS TO SHIELD THEMSELVES FROM THE SUN.

PORCUPINE:

PORCUPINES HAVE SHARP QUILLS THAT CAN DETACH AND GROW
BACK AFTER DEFENDING THEMSELVES.

BUSH PIG:

BUSH PIGS USE THEIR SNOUTS TO DIG FOR ROOTS AND TUBERS.

DUNG BEETLE:

DUNG BEETLES ARE NATURE'S RECYCLERS, THEY HELP CLEAN UP
ANIMAL POOP BY EATING IT! YUCK!

AFRICAN HONEY BEE:

AFRICAN HONEY BEES ARE KNOWN FOR THEIR HIGHLY DEFENSIVE SWARMS.

BUTTERFLY:

BUTTERFLIES TASTE WITH THEIR FEET HAVE COLORFUL WINGS TO HELP THEM HIDE OR WARN PREDATORS..

PRAYING MANTIS:

PRAYING MANTISES CAN TURN THEIR HEADS 180 DEGREES TO SPOT PREY.

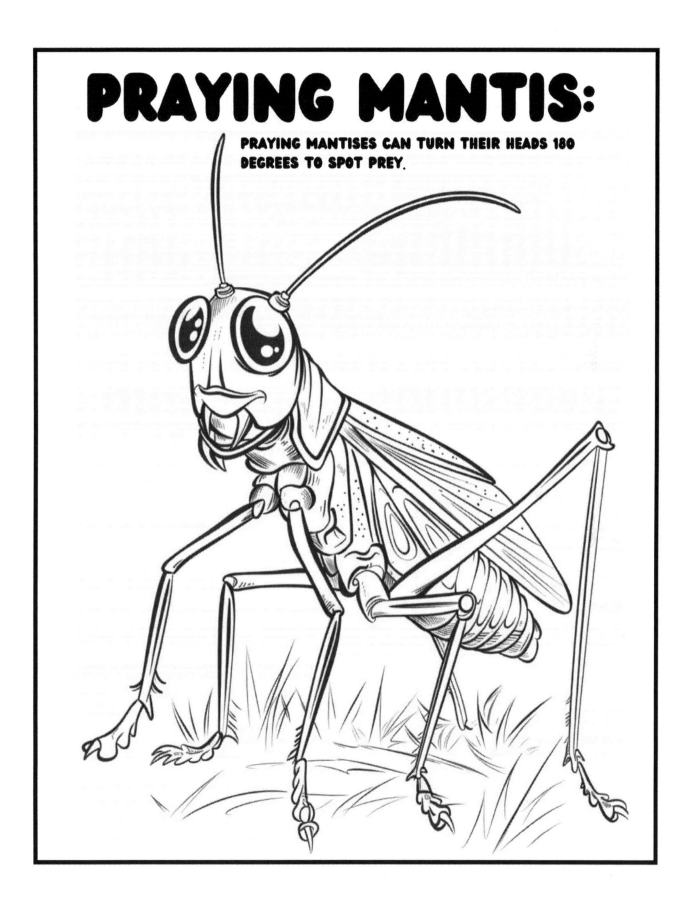

ARMY ANT:

ARMY ANTS BUILD BRIDGES WITH THEIR OWN BODIES AND MARCH TOGETHER LIKE A TINY ARMY.

MILLIPEDE:

DESPITE THE NAME, MILLIPEDES DON'T ACTUALLY HAVE 1,000 LEGS. THEY HAVE AROUND 30-400 DEPENDING ON THE SPECIES!

MOTH:

MOTHS ARE OFTEN MORE ATTRACTED TO UV LIGHT
THAN VISIBLE LIGHT.

DRAGONFLY:

DRAGONFLIES HAVE BEEN AROUND SINCE THE DINOSAURS AND CAN FLY ALL
DIRECTIONS, EVEN BACKWARD, AND HAVE NEARLY 360-DEGREE VISION.

GREAT WHITE SHARK:

GREAT WHITE SHARKS CAN DETECT A SINGLE DROP OF BLOOD IN THE OCEAN FROM MILES AWAY.

PENGUIN:

PENGUINS CAN "FLY" THROUGH WATER AT SPEEDS UP TO 15 MPH.

WHALE: WHALES BREATHE THROUGH A BLOWHOLE ON TOP OF THEIR HEADS.

BULL SHARK:

BULL SHARKS CAN LIVE IN BOTH FRESHWATER RIVERS AND SALTY OCEANS.

MANATEE:

MANATEES ARE OFTEN CALLED "SEA COWS" BECAUSE OF THEIR SLOW, GRAZING BEHAVIOR.

COELACANTH:

COELACANTHS ARE ANCIENT FISH THAT SCIENTISTS THOUGHT
WERE EXTINCT UNTIL THEY WERE REDISCOVERED!

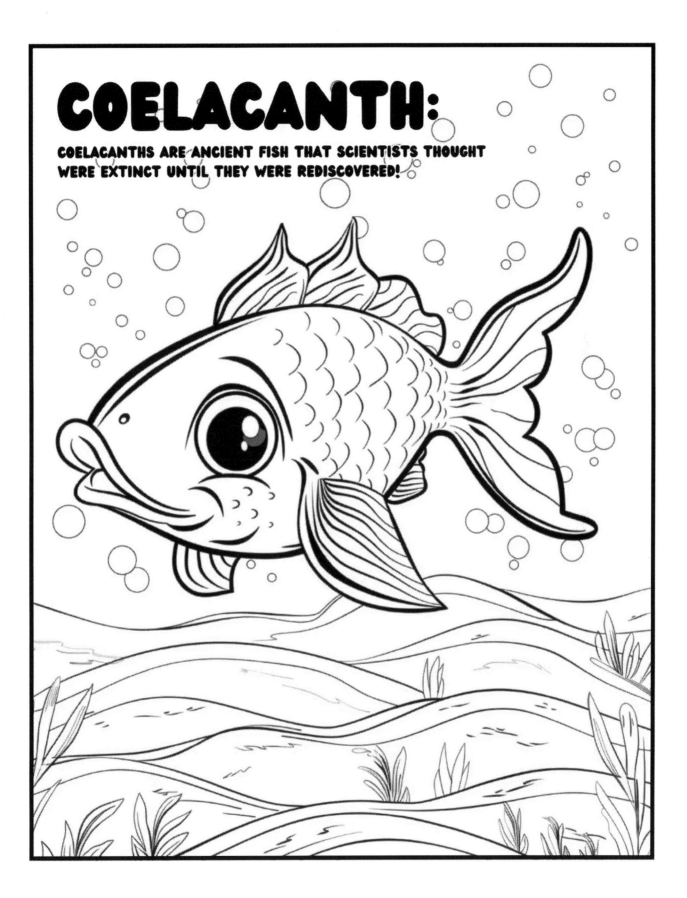

DUGONG:

DUGONGS ARE CLOSELY RELATED TO MANATEES BUT HAVE A DOLPHIN-LIKE TAIL.

NILE PERCH:

NILE PERCH ARE HUGE FRESHWATER FISH THAT CAN GROW AS LONG AS A COUCH.

SHRIMP: SHRIMP'S HEARTS ARE LOCATED IN THEIR HEADS.

TUNA:

TUNA ARE SOME OF THE FASTEST FISH IN THE OCEAN, REACHING SPEEDS UP TO 47 MPH.

DOLPHINS:

DOLPHINS USE ECHOLOCATION TO FIND FOOD AND NAVIGATE.

SEAL:

SEALS USE THEIR WHISKERS TO FEEL VIBRATIONS IN THE WATER AND FIND FOOD.

FENNEC FOX:

FENNEC FOXES HAVE HUGE EARS THAT RADIATE HEAT HELPING THEM STAY COOL IN THE DESERT.

HEDGEHOG:

HEDGEHOGS CURL INTO A BALL, EXPOSING
ONLY THEIR SPIKY QUILLS TO PREDATORS.

WEEVIL:

WEEVILS ARE TINY BEETLES WITH LONG SNOUTS THAT THEY USE TO DRILL INTO SEEDS AND PLANTS TO FIND FOOD!

FROG:

FROGS CAN ABSORB WATER THROUGH THEIR SKIN.

SNAIL:
SNAILS CAN SLEEP FOR UP TO THREE YEARS DURING HIBERNATION.

GREY PARROT:

GREY PARROTS ARE SO SMART THEY CAN SOLVE PUZZLES.

GOLDEN CAT:

AFRICAN GOLDEN CATS ARE ELUSIVE AND RARELY SEEN IN THE WILD.

TURACO:

TURACOS HAVE
FEATHERS WITH A
SPECIAL PIGMENT
THAT MAKES THEM
NATURALLY GREEN.

WILD DONKEY:

WILD DONKEYS CAN SURVIVE WITHOUT WATER FOR LONG PERIODS, RELYING ON MOISTURE FROM PLANTS.

HARRIER HAWK:

HARRIER HAWKS GLIDE CLOSE TO THE
GROUND TO FIND THEIR FOOD.

LUNGFISH:

LUNGFISH CAN SURVIVE OUT OF WATER FOR MONTHS BY BURYING THEMSELVES IN MUD.

Made in the USA
Columbia, SC
14 December 2024

49264956R00050